Buddhism and Christianity

Buddhism and the Vital Problems of Our Time

Two Essays

HELMUTH VON GLASENAPP
*Late Professor of Indology
Tuebingen (Germany)*

BUDDHIST PUBLICATION SOCIETY
Kandy   Sri Lanka

SL ISSN 0049-7541

First Impression: 1959
Second Impression: 1963
Third Impression: 1987

The Wheel Publication No. 16

PREFACE

We are glad to present to our readers another two essays by Prof. Dr. H. von Glasenapp, eminent Indologist of Germany, whose *Vedanta and Buddhism* we published as No. 2 of this series.

The German originals of both these essays appeared in the German magazine, *Universitas*, Vol. IV, No. 1 and V, No. 3, respectively (Stuttgart, 1949, 1950 ; Wissenschaftliche Verlagsgesellschaft, m. b. H.).

The English version of *Buddhism and Christianity*, translated by the Ven. Nyanaponika Mahathera was published first in the *University of Ceylon Review*, Vol. XVI, No. 1 and 2 (Peradeniya, 1958).

The second essay, *Buddhism and the Vital Problems of Our Time*, was originally a radio talk delivered in Munich (Germany), in reply to questions formulated by that broadcasting station. It was later read and discussed at the Indian Institute of Culture, Bangalore. The English version is here reproduced, with amendments, from *The Buddhist*, Vol. XXI, No. 7 (Y.M.B.A., Colombo, 1950).

Both essays give an impartial and scholarly treatment of their respective subjects, and the publishers express the hope that especially the lucid comparison of Buddhism and Christianity will serve to the followers of both religions as a useful source of information about each other's beliefs.

Buddhist Publication Society

BUDDHISM AND CHRISTIANITY

AMONG the five great religions to which nearly nine-tenths of present-day humanity belong, Buddhism and Christianity have been the most frequent subjects of comparison. And rightly so. Because, together with Islam, and unlike Hinduism and Chinese universism, they are "world religions," that is to say, forms of belief that have found followers not merely in a single though vast country, but also in wide regions of the entire world.

Buddhism and Christianity, however, differ from Islam in so far as, unlike the latter, they do not stress the natural aspects of world and man, but they wish to lead beyond them. A comparison between Buddhism and Christianity, however, proves so fruitful mainly because they represent, in the purest form, two great distinctive types of religion which arose East and West of the Indus valley. For two millenniums, these religious systems have given the clearest expression of the metaphysical ideas prevalent in the Far East and in the Occident, respectively.

The similarities between these two religions extend, if I see it rightly, essentially over three spheres : (1) the life history of the founder ; (2) ethics ; and (3) church history.

1, The biographies of Buddha and Christ show many similar features. Both were born in a miraculous way. Soon after their birth, their future greatness is proclaimed by a sage (Asita, Simeon). Both astonish their teachers through the knowledge they possess, though still in their early childhood. Both are tempted by the devil before they start upon their public career. Both walk over the water (*Jātaka*, 190; *Matth.*, 14, 26). Both feed 500 and 5,000 persons, respectively (*Jātaka*, 78 ; *Mark*, 14, 16ff.) by multiplying miraculously the food available. The death of both is accompanied by great natural phenomena. Also the parables ascribed to them show some similarities as, for instance, the story of the sower (*Samyutta*, 42,7 ; *Matth.*, 13, 3), of the prodigal son (*Lotus of the Good Law*, Chap. IV ; *Lk.*, 14), of the widow's mite (*Kalpanamanditika*; *Mark 12*).

From these parallels some writers have attempted to conclude that the Gospels have drawn from the Buddhist texts. But this contention goes much too far. If there is any dependence at all of the stories in the Gospels on those of India, it could be only by oral tradition, through the migration to the West of certain themes which originated in India, and were taken over by the authors of the biblical scriptures. But that is in no way certain, because many of those similarities are not so striking as to exclude the possibility of their independent origin at different places.

2. Both Buddha and Jesus based their ethics on the "Golden Rule." Buddha told the Brahmins and householders of a certain village as follows: "A lay-follower reflects thus : 'How can I inflict upon others what is unpleasant to me ?' On account of that reflection, he does not do any evil to others, and he also does not cause others to do so " (*Samyutta* 55, 7). And Jesus says in the Sermon of the Mount : "Therefore, all things whatsoever ye would that men should do to you, do so to them; for this is the law and the prophets " (*Matth.* 7, 12 ; *Lk.* 6, 31)–this being, by the way, a teaching which, in negative formulation, was already known to the Jewish religion (*Tob.* 15, 4).

Also the principle " Love thy neighbour like unto yourself" (*Lk.* 10, 27) which, in connection with *Lev.* 19, 18, was raised by Jesus to a maxim of ethical doctrine, is likewise found in Buddhism where it was given a philosophical foundation mainly by the thinkers of *Mahāyāna* (Śāntideva, beginning of *Sikṣāsamuccaya*). As to the injunction that love should also be extended to the enemy there is also a parallel statement by the Buddha. According to the *Majjhima Nikāya*, No. 21, he said : "If, O monks, robbers or highwaymen should with a double-handled saw cut your limbs and joints, whoso gave way to anger thereat would not be following my advice. For thus ought you to train yourselves : 'Undisturbed shall our mind remain, no evil words shall escape our lips ; friendly and full of sympathy shall we remain, with heart full of love, free from any hidden malice. And that person shall we suffuse with loving thoughts ; and from there on the whole world."

A practical proof of the love of enemies was given, as the report goes by the Buddhist sage, Āryadeva. After a philosophical disputation, a fanatical adversary attacked him in his cell with a sword, and Āryadeva was fatally wounded. In spite of that, he is said to have helped his murderer to escape by disguising him with his own monk's robe. Schopenhauer, and others after him, believed, in view of these ethical teachings, that the Gospels, "must somehow be of Indian origin" (*parerga* II, sec. 179), and that Jesus was Influenced by Buddhism with which he was said to have become acquainted in Egypt. For such a supposition, however, there is not the slightest reason, since we encounter similar noble thoughts also among Chinese and Greek sages, and, in fact, among the great minds of the whole world, without having to assume an actual interdependence.

3. Also the historical development of both religions presents several parallels. Both, setting out from the countries of their origin, have spread over large parts of the world, but in their original homelands they have scarcely any

followers left. The number of Christians in Palestine is very small today, and on the whole continent of India proper, there are at present not even half a million Buddhists.* The brahmanical counter-reformation starting about 800 A.C., and the onslaught of Islam beginning about 1000 A.C., have brought about the passing of already decadent Buddhism in its fatherland, while it counts millions of devotees in Sri Lanka, Burma, Thailand, China, Japan, Tibet, Mongolia and so on. It is strange how little that fact of the disappearance of Buddhism from the land of the Ganges has been apprised by even many educated persons in the West. Some still believe that Buddhism is the dominant religion of India proper, though out of a population of 400 million, about 95 million belong to the Islam, and 270 million are Hindus (that is devotees of Vishnu and Shiva) among whom the caste system prevails, with Brahmins constituting the hereditary priestly gentry.

It is also significant that today the overwhelming majority of the followers of Buddhism and Christianity belong to a race and linguistic group different from those of their founders. Buddha was an Indo-Aryan ; but, with a few exceptions, most of his devotees are found today among yellow races. Jesus and the Apostles were Jews, but the main contingent of Christians is made up of Europeans speaking Indo-Germanic languages. This shows, very strikingly, that race, language and religion are entirely different spheres. There is perhaps a deep law underlying that fact. Nations of foreign blood accept a new religion with such a great sympathy and enthusiasm probably because it offers them something which they did not possess of their own, and

---

*Since this essay was written, the number of Buddhists in India has increased to an estimated 10—15 million in 1959, mainly due to the mass movement among the scheduled classes initiated by the late Dr. B.R. Ambedkar.—The Editor.

which, therefore, supplements their own mental heritage in an important way. This holds true also in the case of Islam, since among the nearly 300 million Mohammedans, those of the prophet's race, the Semites, are in a minority compared with the Muslims of Turkish, Persian, Indian, Malayan and African extraction.

In the course of their historical development and their dissemination among foreign nations, Buddhism as well as Christianianity have absorbed much that was alien to them at the start. One may even say that, after a religion has gone through a sufficiently long period of development and has been exposed to divers influences, more or less all phenomena will appear which the history of religion has ever produced. Buddhism and Christianity originally had strict views on all matters of sex, but in both certain sects appeared again and again which were given to moral laxity or even taught ritual sex enjoyment, as in Buddhism the Shakti cults of the "Diamond Vehicle" (*Vajrayāna*), or in Christianity certain gnostic schools, medieval sects and modern communities. Buddha and Christ reject extreme asceticism, but there arose numerous zealots who not only advocated painful self-mortification, but even castrated (as the Skopzi) or burned themselves. Pristine Buddhism taught self-liberation through knowledge. Later, however, a school arose which considered man too weak to win salvation by himself, and instead expected deliverance by the grace of Buddha Amitābha. These Amitābha schools have developed a theology which, to a certain extent, presents a parallel to the Protestant doctrine of salvation by faith. In Japan, the most influential of these schools, the Shin sect, has even broken with the principle of monastic celibacy, and thereby, produced a sort of Buddhist clergy of the Protestant type. On the other hand, Tibetan Buddhism has created a kind of ecclesiastical state with the Dalai Lama as its supreme head.

Both Buddhism and Christianity teach the transcending of the world. And, in conformity with the idea of the supremacy of the spiritual life over the conventions of the world, in the monastic order or the church community all class distinctions had to cease. The Buddha taught: "As the rivers lose their names when they reach the ocean, just so members of all castes lose their designaions once they have gone forth into homelessness, following the teaching and the discipline of the Perfect One" (*Aṅg.* 8, 19). And the Apostle Paul wrote (*Gal.* 3, 28): "There is neither Jew nor Greek, there is neither slave nor freeman, neither male nor female, for you are all one in Christ Jesus."

These postulates, however, did not change conditions prevailing in worldly life. Social reforms were entirely alien to the intentions of Buddhism and Christianity in these early days. In various countries and up to modern times, there were not only house slaves, and even temple slaves, but even in Christian countries, slavery was abolished only in the 19th century (Brazil, 1888).

Finally, both religions have in common certain features of cult and forms of worship. I mention here only: monasticism, tonsure of the clergy, confession, the cult of images, relic worship, ringing of bells, use of rosary and incense, and the erection of towers. There has been much controversy about the question whether, and to what extent, one may assume mutual influence with regard to these and several other similarities, but research has so far not come to an entirely satisfactory conclusion.

Though in many details there are great similarities between Buddhism and Christianity, one must not overlook the fact that in matters of doctrine they show strong contrasts, and their conceptions of salvation belong to entirely different types of religious attitude. Buddhism, in its purest form, presents a religion based on the conception of an eternal and universal law, a conception found in various forms in India, China and Japan. Christianity, on the other hand, belongs, together with the teaching of Zoroaster, the Jewish religion and Islam, to those religions that profess to have a divine revelation which is manifested in history, and these religions have conquered for themselves all parts of the world west of India. The contrast between Buddhism and Christianity will become clear by objectively placing side by side their central doctrines. I shall base that comparison on what are still today, just as nearly 2,000 years ago, the fundamental doctrinal tenets of both religions, and shall not consider here differences of detail or modern interpretations. Since I may assume an acquaintance with the teaching of Christianity, I shall begin each subsequent discussion of single points with a very brief statement of the Christian doctrine concerned, following it up with a somewhat more detailed treatment of the different teachings in Buddhism. I hope that in that way I shall be able to bring out clearly the differences between these two religions.

1. Christianity differs from all great world religions first of all in that it gives to the personality of its founder a central position in world history as well as in the doctrine of salvation. In Buddhism, Zoroastrianism, Islam, Judaism, and still more so in religions having no personal founder but being products of historical growth, like Hinduism and Chinese universism, in all of them it is a definite metaphysical and ethical doctrine promulgated by holy men which is the very centre of their systems. For the Christian, however, it is faith in Jesus Christ that is the inner core of his religion. This evinces most clearly from the fact alone that the 22 scriptures of the New Testament contain only comparatively

few sermons of Jesus concerned with doctrinal matters, while by far the greatest part of the Buddhist Canon is devoted to expositions of the Buddha's teachings. In the scriptures of the New Testament, from the Gospel of St. Matthew up to the Revelation of St. John, the most important concern of the authors was to demonstrate that Christ was a supernatural figure unique in the entire history of the world. Christ's redemptory death on the cross, his resurrection, ascension, and his future advent are, therefore, the core of the Christian doctrine of salvation.

Buddha's position in Buddhist doctrine bears in no way comparison with those features of Christianity. For the historical Gautama was not the incarnation of a God; he was a human being, purified through countless rebirths as animal, man or angel, until finally in his last embodiment, he attained by his own strength that liberating knowledge which enabled him to enter Nirvāna. He was one who pointed out the way to deliverance, but did not, by himself, bestow salvation on others. Though also to him a miraculous birth has been attributed, yet it was not described as a virginal birth. The whole difference, however, of the Buddha's status from that of Christ is chiefly demonstrated by the fact that a Buddha is not an isolated historical phenomenon, but that many Enlightened Ones had appeared in the past, teaching the same doctrine; and that in the future, too, Buddhas will appear in the world who will expound to erring humanity the same principles of deliverance in a new form. The later Buddhism of the Great Vehicle (*Mahāyāna*) even teaches that many if not all men carry within themselves the seed of Buddhahood, so that after many rebirths they themselves will finally attain the highest truth and impart it to others.

2. But even the historical personalities of Jesus and the Buddha differ widely. Jesus grew up in a family of poor Jewish craftsmen. Devoting himself exclusively to religious

questions, he was a successor of the Jewish prophets who enthusiastically proclaimed the divine inspirations bestowed upon them. As a noble friend of mankind, full of compassion for the poor, he preached gentleness and love for one's neighbour ; but, on the other hand, he attacked with a passionate zeal abuses, for instance when he showed up as hypocrites the Scribes and Pharisees, when he drove from the Temple the traders and money-lenders, and held out the prospect of eternal damnation to those who refused to believe in him (*Mark* 16, 16). With the conviction of being the expected Messiah he preached the early advent of the Heavenly kingdom (*Matth.* 10, 23). With that promise he primarily turned to the "poor in spirit" (*Matth.* 5, 3), because not speculative reasoning, but pious and deep faith is the decisive factor: What is hidden to the clever and wise, has been revealed by God to the babes (*Matth.* 11, 25).

Gautama Buddha, however, stemmed from the princely house of the Sakyas that reigned on the southern slopes of the Himalaya. He lived in splendour and luxury up to his 29th year, when he left the palace and its womanfolk and went forth into homelessness as a mendicant. After a six years' vain quest for insight spent with various Brahman ascetics, he won enlightenment at Uruvela. This transformed the Bodhisattva. *i. e.*, an aspirant for enlightenment, into a Buddha, that is into one who has awakened to truth. From then onward, up to the eightieth year of his life, he proclaimed the path of deliverance found by him. He died at Kusinārā about 480 B. C. Buddha was an aristocrat of high culture, with a very marked sense for beauty in nature and art, free from any resentment, and possessed of a deep knowledge of man's nature. He was a balanced personality, with a serene mind and winning manners, representing the type of a sage who, with firm roots within, had risen above the world.

In the struggle with the systems of his spiritually dynamic time, he evolved out of his own thought a philosophical system that made high demands on the mental faculties of his listeners. As he himself said : "My doctrine is for the wise and not for the unwise." The fact that his teaching had an appeal also for the uneducated is explained by his great skill in summarizing in easily intelligible language the fundamental ideas of his philosophy.

So far we have found the following difference between Buddhism and Christianity: Christianity, from its very start was a *movement of faith* appealing to the masses; only when it won over the upper classes did a Christian philosophy evolve. Buddhism, however, was in its beginnings a *philosophical teaching of deliverance*. Its adherents were mainly from the classes of noblemen and warriors and the wealthy middle-class, with a few Brahmins. Only when Buddhism reached wider circles did it become a popular religion.

3. The teaching of all great religions are laid down in holy scriptures to which an authoritative character is ascribed surpassing all other literature. Christianity regards the Bible as the "Word of God," as an infallible source of truth in which God, by inspiring the authors of these scriptures, revealed things that otherwise would have remained hidden to man. Contrary to Christianity, Islam and Hinduism, atheistic Buddhism does not know of a revelation in that sense. Nevertheless, it possesses a great number of holy texts in which the sayings of the Buddha are collected. That Canon comprises those insights which the Buddha is said to have won by his own strength through comprehending the true nature of reality. It is claimed that everyone who, in his mental development, reaches the same high stage of knowledge will find confirmed by himself the truth of the Buddha's statements. In fact, however, Buddhists ascribe to

that Canon likewise a kind of revealing character, in so far as they appeal to the sayings of the "omniscient" Buddha which are regarded by them as the final authority. The interpretation of the Buddha word, however, has led among Buddhists to as many controversies as Bible exegesis among Christians.

We shall now proceed to describe the fundamental tenets of Christian and Buddhist doctrine. In doing so, we shall have to limit ourselves to the general principles which, for two thousand years, have been common to all schools or denominations of these religions. I shall first speak about the different position taken by Christians and Buddhists towards the central questions of religion, that is God, world and soul, and later proceed to a treatment of their teachings on salvation.

4. The central tenet of Christian doctrine is the belief in an eternal, personal, omnipotent, omniscient and all-loving God. He has created the world from nothing, sustains it, and directs its destiny; he is law-giver, judge, the helper in distress and the saviour of the creatures which he has brought into being. Angels serve him to carry out his will. As originally created by God, all of them were good angels. But a section of them turned disobedient, and breaking away from the heavenly hosts, formed an opposition to the other angels, a hierarchy which under its leader, Satan, strives to entice man to evil. Though the devil's power is greater than that of man, it is restricted by the power of God so that they cannot do anything without God's consent, and at the end of the days they will be subjected to divine judgement.

Buddhists, on their part, believe in a great number of deities (*devatā*) which direct the various manifestations of nature and of human life. They also know of evil demons and of a kind of devil, *Māra*, who tries to turn the pious from the path of virtue. But all these beings are impermanent though their life span may last millions of years. In the course of their rebirths they have come to their superhuman form of existence thanks to their own deeds; but when the productive power of their deeds is exhausted, they have to be reborn on earth again, as humans. Though the world will always have a sun god or a thunder god, the occupants of these positions will change again and again in the course of time. It is obvious that these gods with their restricted life span, range of action and power, cannot be compared with the Christian God since they cannot, be it singly or in their totality, create the world or give it its moral laws. Hence they resemble only powerful superhuman kings whom the pious devotees may well, to a certain extent, solicit for gifts and favours, but who cannot exert any influence on world events in their totality.

Many Hindus assume that, above the numerous impermanent deities, exists an eternal, omniscient, all-loving and omnipotent God who creates, sustains, rules and destroys the world. But the Buddhists deny the existence of such a Lord of the Universe because, according to them, in the first place, no such original creator of the world can be proved to exist, since every cause must have another cause; and secondly, an omnipotent God will also have to be the creator of evil and this will conflict with his all-loving nature; or, alternatively, if he is to be good and benevolent, he will have to be thought of without omnipotence and omniscience, since otherwise he would not have called into existence this imperfect world of suffering or he would have eliminated evil. Buddhism, therefore, is outspokenly atheistic in that respect. The world is not governed by a personal God, but by an impersonal law which, with inexorable consistency, brings retribution for every morally good or evil deed. The idea that there are numerous deities of limited power can be found also in other religions; and the ancient Greeks, Romans and Germans believed that, above the gods, there is Moira, Anangke, Fatum or Destiny, which eventually rules everything. For the Chinese the highest principle is the "Tao" which sustain the cosmic order and the harmony between heaven, earth and man. With the Indians there appears already in Vedic times the idea that gods and men are subject to the moral word-order, the Rita, and from about 800 B.C. this idea is linked with the doctrine of *Karma*, the doctrine of the after-effects of guilt and merit. According to that doctrine, every action carries in itself, seed-like, its own reward punishment. After death, an individual, in accordance with his good or evil deeds, is reincarnated in the body of either an animal, a man, a deity or a demon, in order to reap the fruits of his previous actions. This retribution occurs automatically, as a natural, regular occurrence, without requiring a divine judge who shares out reward and punishment.

As to the differences between Buddhism and Christianity, in the present context, we may say that the same functions which in Christian doctrine are related to the concept of a personal God are in Buddhism divided among a number of different factors. The natural and moral order of the world and its periodical rise and fall are preserved by an impersonal and immanent comic law (*Dharma*). The retribution for one's actions operates through the inherent efficacy of these deeds themselves. Helpers in need are the numerous but transient deites, while the truths of deliverance are revealed by human beings evolved to the perfection of Buddhas (Awakened Ones), who therefore are also made objects of a cult and of devotion. Saviour, however, is each man for himself, in so far as he has overcome the world through wisdom and self-control.

The homage paid to the Buddha, as it may be observed in Buddhist temples, has a meaning quite different from the worship of God in Christian Churches. The Christian worships God in reverence due to the creator of the universe and the ruler of all its destinies ; or he does so in order to be granted spiritual or material boons by God's grace. The Buddhist pays homage to the Buddha without expecting that he hears him or does something for him. Since the Buddha has entered into Nirvāna he can neither hear the prayers of the pious nor can he help them. If a Buddhist turns to the Buddha as if to a personality that actually confronts him, his act has a fictive character. The devotee expects from his act only spiritual edification and a good Karma. This theory as advocated today by orthodox Buddhism has, however, often been altered in practice and in the teachings of some of the Buddhist schools. But even those who think it possible that a Buddha may intervene in favour of a devotee regard the Buddha only as a saviour, a bringer of deliverance, and not as the creator and ruler of the universe.

5. According to Christian doctrine, God has created the world from nothing, and he rules it according to a definite plan. The stopping of the cosmic process comprises the end of the world, the universal resurrection of the dead, the Day of Judgement, the eternal damnation of the sinners and the eternal bliss of the pious in a heavenly Jeresalem descended to earth. Until the 18th century, it was belived that the entire world history comprised only 6,000 years, though the time of the creation has been calculated differently. The Byzantines made their world era start on the Ist of

September, 5509 B.C., while Luther dated the creation at the year 3960 B.C. Although the calculations about the beginning and the end of the world process—mainly based on the statements about the generations between Adam and Christ (*Matth.*, 1, 17 and *Lk*, 3, 21)—have been abandoned in recent times, yet for Christianity the view that the historical fact of creation and salvation constitutes a single and unrepeatable event, remains a guiding principle.

Buddhism, however, knows neither a first beginning nor a definite end of the world. Since every form of existence presupposes action in a preceding life, and since karma produced in one existence must find its retribution in a future one, Buddhism teaches a periodical cycle of cosmic rise and fall, evolution and dissolution. Since the number of living beings that produce karma, is infinitely vast, and the unexhausted karma, of beings inhabiting a world which is in the process of dissolution has to find realization in a newly arising world, worldly existence will never come to an end, however large the number of human beings may be that reach deliverance. There is another essential difference between the Christian and the Buddhist conception of the world. Buddhists have always assumed an infinite number of world systems situated next to each other in space, each of them consisting of an earth, a heaven above and a hell below.

6. According to Christian views, man is composed of body and soul. While the body is formed of matter in the mother's womb, the soul is a special creation of God, from nothing. A soul is a simple, spiritual, immaterial substance. Maintained in eternal existence by God, the soul continues also after the dissolution of the body at death and receives from God the rewards of its deeds, either in heaven or hell. At the end of time, God causes a resurrection of all flesh

and unites again the souls with their former bodies. By the fact that thus the whole man, i. e., not only his soul but also his body, receives reward or punishment, the bliss of the heavenly realm or the torment of eternal of damnation is felt with still greater intensity. In Christianity, the significance of life on earth, and of the decisions made in it, has been enhanced to the utmost through the idea that it is man's conduct during that short life-span which determines the soul's destiny for all eternity.

Also many Indian systems are based upon that anthropological dualism. It is the conception of an infinitely large number of eternal and purely spiritual souls linked, since beginningless time, with bodies formed by particles of primordial matter. The souls are thought to change these bodies in the course of their existences, until they become free of them on attainment of deliverance. In contrast to all Indian teachings of deliverance, and most others, Buddhism denies the existence of eternal substances, essentially unchangeable. What appears to us as matter, actually comes into being only through the natural co-operation of a multitude of single factors like colours, sounds, odours, tactiles, spatial and temporal qualities, etc. Also what we call "soul" is only a play of ever-changing sensations, perceptions and cognitive acts, combined into an entirety, yet being devoid of any underlying entity. It is only because some of these complex phenomena seem to have a relative stability that men believe in the existence of matter or soul. But in truth, only *dharmas* exist, i. e., "factors of existence" that arise in functional dependence on each other, and cease again after a short time. This doctrine of the *dharmas* is the characteristic teaching peculiar to Buddhism. It was developed by the Buddha into a philosophy of becoming from an idea still noticeable in the Vedic texts ascribing positive subsistence to everything that exists including qualities, events, modal states, etc.

In that respect, Buddha is a precursor of Hume and Mach who likewise declared any substance to be a fiction. But for the Buddha, the doctrine of the *dharmas* combines with the acceptance of a moral law governing the efficacy of all actions. Just as nothing occurs without producing some effect in the physical world, so every morally good or evil act is the cause of definite effects. Though when a being dies a combination of factors is dissolved which had previously formed a personality, yet the deeds performed in the life now passed become the cause of a new and separate being's birth. The newly born is different from the being that had died, but it takes over, as it were, the latter's inheritance. Thus the stream of the factors of existence is continued also after death, and one life form follows the other without break. Since any act can have only a retribution of limited duration, Buddhists do not know eternal bliss in heaven or eternal torments in hell, but believe that the inhabitants of heaven and hell are later reborn again on earth.

7. Christianity and Buddhism agree in their strong emphasis on the impermanency of all things. In Christianity, the suffering inherent in the world is the outcome of sin, and sin is disobedience towards God's commandments. Because Adam had sinned, all his progeny is afflicted with Orginal Sin. Man is too weak to free himself from sin by his own strength. Therefore God in his compassion became man in Christ, and died as a vicarious redemptory sacrifice for all humanity. Through Christ's sacrificial death all men have become free from the power of sin, but that vicarious salvation from evil becomes reality only if man opens himself to divine grace through his faith in Christ.

The idea of collective guilt and collective salvation is far from the Buddhist's way of thinking. According to Buddhism, everyone accumulates his own evil and everyone has to work out his own deliverance. The entire Christian conception of sin, as a matter of fact, is alien to the Buddhist. If man has to suffer in punishment for his misdeeds, it is not on account of his disobeying divine commandments, but because his actions are in conflict with the eternal cosmic law and, therefore, produce bad karma. In general, the suffering which is life for a Buddhist is not stamped with the mark of sin, but carries only the character of impermanence and insubstantiality. This inherent characteristic of existence is the cause of life ever ending in death, of life with its aimless and meaningless wandering through always new forms of being. It is that which basically constitutes life's suffering. And the cause of this woeful conflict is a thirst for sense enjoyment, an attachment to existence, a will to live, a passion that either craves for possession or wants to escape. All these propensities and impulses have their original source in ignorance, that is, in lack of insight into the true nature of reality. He who sees that neither in the internal nor in the external world can anything be found that abides ; and that there is also no ego as a point of rest within the general flux of phenomena ; who is aware that there is no self either as the eternal witness or temporary owner of sense perceptions and volitions—such a one, through that very knowledge, is set free of selfishness, of hate, greed and delusion. By a gradual process of purification, extending through aeons over many existences, he finally discards the illusion of self-affirmation. Through mindful observation, keen reflection and meditative calm he eliminates all selfish propensities, and sees also his own personality as a mere bundle of *dharmas*, i e , processes of natural law that arise and vanish conditioned by functional relations. Dispassionate and without attachment, he pervades, as the Buddhist scriptures say, "the whole world with his heart filled with loving-kindness, compassion, sympathetic joy and equanimity" (*Digha* No. 3). Without clinging to life and without fear of death he waits for the hour when his bodily form breaks up and he reaches final deliverance from rebirth.

8. The definite and perpetual state of salvation which is the redeemed person's share according to Christian doctrine is conceived as an eternal life in the heavenly kingdom. If, after the second advent of Christ, the resurrection of the dead and the Last Judgement, the final kingdom of God has been established, then, after the old world's destruction, on a new earth, the redeemed ones will live in an inseparable communion with God and Christ.

The Buddhist conception of Nirvāna presents the most radical contrast to Christian eschatology. The Christian hopes for infinite continuation of his entire personality, not only of his soul but also of his body resurrected from dust to a new life. The Buddhist, however, wishes to be extinguished completely, so that all mental and corporeal factors which form the individual will disappear without a remainder. Nirvāna is the direct opposite of all that constitutes earthly existence. It is a relative Naught in so far as it contains neither the consciousness nor any other factor that occurs in this world of change or could possibly contribute to its formation. Not wrongly, therefore, has Nirvāna been compared to empty space in which there are no differentiations left, and which does not cling to anything. In strongest contrast to the world which is impermanent, without an abiding self-nature and subject to suffering, Nirvāna is highest bliss, but a bliss that is not *felt*, i.e., beyond the happiness of sensation (*Aṅg.* 9, 34, 1-3). In the conception of the final goal of deliverance there is expressed the ultimate and most decisive contrast between the Christian and the Buddhist abnegation of the world The Christian renounces the world because it is imperfect through sin, and he hopes for a personal, active and eternal life beyond, in a world which, through God's power, has been freed from sin and purified to perfection. But the Buddhist thinks that an individual existence without becoming and cessation, and hence without suffering, is unthinkable. He believes though, that in future, during the ever-recurring cyclical changes of good and bad epochs, also a happy age will dawn upon mankind again. But that happy epoch will be no less transient than earlier ones have been. Never will the cosmic process find its crowning consummation in a blessed finality. Hence there is no collective salvation, but only an individual deliverance. While the cosmic process following unalterable laws continues its course, only a saint who has become mature for Nirvāna will extinguish like a flame without fuel, in the midst of an environment that, with fuel un-exhausted, is still aburning.

9. The different attitude towards the world and its history tallies also with the dissimilar evaluation given to other religions by Christians and Buddhists respectively. Christianity, being convinced of the absolute superiority of its own faith, has always questioned the justification of other forms of faith. Buddhism, however, does not believe that man has to decide about it within a single life on earth. The Buddhist, therefore, regards all other religions as first steps to his own. Consequently, in the countries to which Buddhism spread, it did not fight against the original religions found there, but tried to suffuse them with its own spirit. Therefore, Buddhism has never claimed exclusive, absolute

or totalitarian authority. In modern China most Buddhists are simultaneously Confucians and Taoists, and in Japan membership in a Buddhist sect does not exclude faith in the Shinto gods. This large-heatred tolerance of Buddhism is also illustrated in its history, which is almost free from religious wars and persecution of heretics.

The fundamental doctrines of Buddhism and Christianity as outlin d here and accepted as concrete facts by the majority of the faithful have sometimes been interpreted by thinkers of both religions in a rationalistic or in a mystical sense, and these interpretations have modified the meaning of these doctrines considerably. In our present context, however, we cannot enter into a treatment of these transformations. By doing so, our comparative study would lack that firm ground required, which, for a historian's purpose, can be provided only by the authoritative and clearly outlined tenets of the respective teachings.

Though Buddhism and Christianity differ from each other in their respective views about world and self, about the meaning of life and man's ultimate destiny, yet they agree again in the ultimate postulates of all religious life. For both religions proclaim man's responsibility for his actions and the freedom of moral choice; both teach retribution for all deeds, and believe in the perfectibility of the individual. "You must be perfect as your Father in Heaven is perfect" (*Matth.* 5, 48), says Jesus. And the Buddha summarizes the essence of his ethics in the words : "To shun all evil, to practise what is good, to cleanse one's own heart : that is the teaching of the Enlightened Ones."

BUDDHISM AND THE VITAL PROBLEMS OF OUR TIME

Buddhism venerates as its founder the Indian Prince Siddhartha of the family of the Shakyas (c. 560–480 B. C.), whom his contemporaries were accustomed to call by his surname Gautama or by the honorific "Buddha." The word Buddha means the Awakened, the Enlightened, and was applied to the Indian men of those times who were believed to have fathomed the mystery of the world and to have discovered the way to salvation by their own efforts and not through revelation. The gospel of Gautama spread quickly over the whole of India in his lifetime and after his death, but fell into decay by about 100 A.D., and had to give way, in the country of its origin, to Hinduism and Islam.

But Buddhism found ample recompense for this loss in Sri Lanka and Further India, in China, Japan, Tibet and Mongolia. The number of Buddhists in the Far East is estimated at 500 to 600 million, but this figure does not give a clear idea of its extension, since the acceptance of some of its doctrines or the observance of Buddhist customs is not incompatible with adhesion to Confucianism, Taoism, Shinto and the various popular cults. For it has always been foreign to the spirit of Buddhism to claim exclusive validity. On the contrary, in its all-embracing tolerance, it has always lived peacefully side by with other religions, and has absorbed ideas originally foreign to it, trying to permeate them with its own spirit.

Present-day Buddhism flourishes in two different forms. In Sri Lanka and Further India the original doctrine prevails, which is called the Lesser Vehicle, or *Hīnayāna*; in the Far East and the Tibetan cultural area this "simple doctrine" has undergone a significant broadening as regards philosophy and ceremonial. This is called the Great Vehicle to salvation, *Mahāyāna*. But the basic ideas of all forms of Buddhism have remained more or less the same, so that in our survey we need take no notice of the differences in detail.

Among the world religions, Buddhism is the one whose area of influence lies farthest from the West, and also that which is most different in its doctrine from the teachings of Christianity and Islam.

God

First and foremost, Buddhism does not teach the existence of any personal god who created and rules the world. It admits the existence of many gods; but these are only transitory beings with limited powers. They are born and pass away; they can exert no influence on the world process as a whole. Also the great saints and saviours, the Buddhas and Bodhisattvas, do not have the position which the Western religions ascribe to their one God. They can enlighten individuals, and according to the Great Vehicle can lead them by their grace to the path of salvation. But they are not able to interfere with the cosmic process or change the world.

The universe follows its own unalterable natural and moral laws. The most important of these is the law of karma, the law of retributive moral causality. This brings it about that every ethically good or bad action inexorably finds its rewards or punishment, because the doer of the deed is born again after his death as a new being, and in that life reaps what he has sown in the previous life.

The Soul

Another point on which Buddhism differs from Christianity and Islam is this: both Western religions assume immortal souls created by God, which, after death continue to exist in heaven or hell. Buddhism, however, denies that there can be anything in the world which persists unchanged. According to its theory, life is a stream of elements which are always coming into existence and ceasing to exist, which influence each other according to certain laws. The life-stream of man continues after his death as a new being which has to pursue its happy and unhappy existence, as god, man, animal or inhabitant of hell, in accordance with the good or evil nature of his deeds. A life continues until the karma, the power of the deeds which called the being into existence, is exhausted. Then, on the basis of the actions performed in that life, a new being comes into existence which is the heir of the previous life, and so on.

Since each life is the consequence of the actions of a previous life, no beginning of the world can be conceived. Since in each life new actions are performed which produce karma, there can in the natural course of things be no end of the world. A few beings, however, succeed, through knowledge of truth, in getting rid of the passions which are the root cause of the karmic process. They withdraw from the world, they enter into Nirvāna, into the great peace. But, however many beings may enter into Nirvāna, the cosmic process will never come to an end. For the number of beings who inhabit the infinitely vast number of worlds as animals, men, spirits, gods and inhabitants of hell, is infinitely great.

Thus as little can be said about an end of the world as about a beginning. And with this we come to at hird important point where Buddhism differs from Islam and Christianity. Both of these teach that the world was created by God out of nothing, that it remains under his governance for some thousands of years and that on the Last Day it will come to a definite end, when the dead will rise again, all men will receive their eternal reward or eternal punishment, and a new earth of eternal duration and splendour will be created. The ideas of a primordial creation and a definite end of the world are as foreign to Buddhism as that of a providential direction of cosmic events in accordance with a divine plan. It will be evident that, because of these divergences from the conceptions and dogmas of theistic religions, Buddhism must strive at different answers concerning many of the questions which concern us here.

Before I proceed to discuss these questions, I must say a word about my own personal attitude towards Buddhism. I am not a Buddhist, but one engaged in Buddhist research. I have concerned myself for over thirty years with the Buddhist scriptures in the Indian languages, and have studied the principal Buddhist countries (except Tibet and Mongolia) at first-hand on three prolonged visits. In view of my knowledge of the Buddhist sacred writings, and the many discussions I have had with Buddhist monks and laymen, I believe I can answer these questions objectively and correctly in the spirit of Buddhism. I hope that in this way I shall be able to add to the understanding of a doctrine the study of which has been my life's work, and a knowledge of which, in my opinion, is necessary for anybody who seriously concerns himself with the various solutions which the riddle of existence puts before us.

The Meaning of Life

(1) The first question which has been addressed to me is : "So far as we can see, both the life of the individual, and the history of mankind, as a whole, proceed according to definite laws and in definite phases. Apart from such causal regularities, has life any *meaning* which is comprehensible to us? Has man any definite task within this world?

Or does this task merely consist in preparing himself to leave the world?

"Regarded from the religious standpoint, is it ultimately unimportant how man behaves in this world? If not, where can he find directions as to his behaviour, and how can he know the validity of these directions? If the world has a comprehensible meaning, how is the suffering of innocent people to be explained?"

As I see it, there are in this group of questions no fewer than six separate questions. I shall answer them one by one.

(a) What is the goal of the cosmic process? According to the Buddhist view, which I have already outlined, this question cannot be answered. For Buddhism does not believe in a final state of things towards which histore progresses. The cosmos is in eternal movement, and the numerous world systems of which it consists pass periodically through the four phases of coming into being, existence, dissolution and non-existence.

Cosmology

Buddhist cosmology usually starts by describing how an existing world which is ripe for dissolution is emptied of its inhabitants. These beings, after their death, are born again in another world, and the uninhabited world is destroyed completely by fire, water or wind. The world thus destroyed disappears for an enormous period of time, and there exists in its place only empty space. When the lawfully fixed period of non-existence comes to an end, there arises a new world system by virtue of the latent karmic power of the beings of the world which was destroyed. In empty space there first springs up a faint breeze which grows ever stronger and finally the heaven worlds, earth and hell are formed. These are then populated with the beings who have had to live through the intervening period in other worlds.

At the beginning of such a newly arisen world, men are without sex. They are endowed with a radiant body, they hover over the earth's surface, and they need no physical nourishment. But because out of curiosity they feed on the finer substance of the earth, they become earth-bound creatures with gross and perishable bodies. Desire which grows ever stronger in them causes them gradually to lose their original purity and virtue ; they give themselves to bodily pleasures and quarrel with each other over their possessions which had so far been held in common. So that order may be re-established, property is introduced, and one man is installed as king. The need for a division of labour then leads to the formation of special callings and castes.

Over a period of millions of years, the natural and moral condition of the world deteriorates from generation to generation, so that human beings who in the beginning had an unimaginably long life, now never live beyond a hundred years. This position in which we find ourselves now will in the future become still worse. At last Armageddon, "the time of the swords," breaks out, which lasts for seven days, during which the greater part of mankind is killed.

During this period of horror a few men have gone back to live in the forest and subsist peacefully on fruit and roots. Taught by the catastrophe, they determine for the future to live a peaceful, moral life. Henceforth conditions improve so that men become good and happy. This better state of things again lasts only for a time, and then decline sets in. Twenty periods of this kind, of falling and rising culture, follow in succession. When in the last, the twentieth period, the optimal point is reached, an emptying of the world from all living beings takes place, and finally its destruction, as described before. In this manner the cosmos undergoes continuous change, as in accordance with eternal laws, many worlds, one after another, come into existence and pass away.

(*b*) Thus Buddhism knows no ultimate goal of world evolution. Nevertheless, the world has a meaning. It is the ever-changing scene of the retribution of good and evil deeds (*karma*).

(*c*) The duty of man consists, in the first place, to see to it that through leading a moral life he is reborn in a good environment, with a happy future. As a distant and supreme goal Nirvāna beckons to the religious man, but it can be attained only after long purification. Hence the final task of man is to prepare himself to leave the world.

(*d*) From the foregoing it follows that according to the Buddhist view the present conduct of man is of fundamental importance for his future fate. The entire Buddhist teaching is based on a belief in the moral structure of the universe. Such a belief rests not only on the conviction that everything good and evil will have its retribution and that it is possible for man continually to perfect himself, it also presupposes that there exists an objective criterion of what helps man on the way to perfection and of what obstructs his progress.

The Buddha proclaimed an ethics of intention. What decides whether an action produces good or bad karma is the intention with which it is performed. Therefore, actions which are not performed as the result of a moral decision, positive or negative, have no karmic results.

It is understandable that this lofty philosophical view was not preserved for long. In the course of its history Buddhism has developed, in many different forms, the theory that the giving of gifts to monks, and the performance of certain sacred rites, produce a store of meritorious works. Indeed, in many of the schools of the Great Vehicle, ritualism has obtained such importance that the performance of magical rites, like the mechanical turning of prayer-wheels or the muttering of certain sacred formulae, has become a principal activity of the devotees. This is a regrettable though understandable degeneration, which, indeed, is not unknown in other religions.

Rebirth

(*e*) For the doctrine that good or evil deeds receive their reward or punishment in a new existence, Buddhists find empirical confirmation in this, that according to their opinion, men who have reached a certain height of spiritual development are able to look back upon their own previous lives and the rebirths of other beings. Since only a few individuals have reached so high a stage of spiritual maturity, the rest of us must rely on the testimony of these saints, just as those who have not visited a foreign country have to put their trust in the statement of reliable travellers.

First among possessors of such knowledge come the Buddhas, i. e., men to whom, by virtue of the enlightenment they have attained, the connection between natural events and the moral realm has become evident. The word of a Buddha, therefore, ranks as the highest authority for all conduct; and from the sayings of Gautama preserved in the holy scriptures, a Buddhist derives guidance for his life.

(*f*) The doctrine of moral causality offers the Buddhists an explanation why one man is distinguished, rich and happy, and the other lowly, poor and miserable. The fact that good men often fare badly, while evil men are happy, is explained according to this doctrine by assuming that the good men have still to expiate in this life the sins of a previous existence while a bad man who has done good deeds in his previous life is now getting the reward for them. For the whole of the circumstances in which anyone now lives is a consequence of the actions of his previous existence, while on the other hand, what he does now is done by the free decision of his will.

It can be objected against this theory that in his behaviour man is very largely determined by his predispositions, and that it is therefore difficult to establish the freedom of his moral decisions. Buddhism replies on this point that, against the fatalistic teachings of his time, the Buddha always emphasised : "I teach (the efficacy of) action and energy," and that the workings of the law of karma are beyond the grasp of the ordinary man.

(2) The second question which I have to answer from the standpoint of Buddhism runs thus : "If man has a normative ideal to which he has to conform, what are the conditions of life which guarantee him the quickest fulfilment of this task ?"

According to the Buddhist view, man occupies an exceptional position among living beings. He alone is in a position to question life itself and to achieve a transcending of it. Animals cannot do so, since they are wholly absorbed by the life of the senses. The heavenly beings also cannot do so, since because of their long life and the happiness they enjoy, the idea never occurs to them that life is transient and, therefore, unsubstantial and unsatisfactory.

In consequence of this middle position in the hierarchy of living forms which man occupies, existence as a man is always praised as a rare piece of good fortune. On this point it is said : "The chance is as small as that a blind turtle, emerging from the sea once in a hundred years, should put its head straight into a single-necked yoke—so small is the chance that a being in the course of his repeated rebirth should once become a man" *(Majjhima,* No. 159*).*

Man should, therefore, make use of the precious boon which has fallen to his lot, and take care that he improves himself morally, in order gradually to attain perfection. A famous saying in the *Dhammapada* (v. 183) shows the way to the fulfilment of this task : "Shun all evil, do good, and purify your own heart : that is the teacing of the Buddhas." The avoidance of evil consists in not killing, not stealing, not lying, not committing fornication and not using intoxicating drinks, which reduce man's mental capacity or deaden his sense of responsibility. He should, therefore, follow no calling in which he is bound to come into conflict with these postulates ; he cannot be a hunter, a butcher, an executioner, a publican, and so on. It is easiest for him if he detaches himself from the world, and thus avoids its temptations. But only a few are mature enough to enter the monastery or to live as pious hermits.

Thus the Buddhist ought not to be content with conditions as he finds them ; he must try, wherever he can, to change them in accordance with Buddhist principles. Where that is not possible, his effort must be to make himself inwardly free from his environment so that he may detach himself from it and rise above it.

(3) We now come to the third question which raises the following problem :

"Are all men equal? If not, in what do they differ? In what respects is equality of all men desirable, and how far should existing differences be preserved?"

Since not even twins are completely alike in their abilities and their destiny, there can be in practice no complete equality of all men. Buddhism has, therefore, never tried to make all men alike. According to Buddhism mankind as a whole resembles to a certain extent a great pyramid, the broad base of which consists of the crude worldlings who are still far removed from the light of truth, while the narrow summit comprises only the few perfected ones. And between these two extremes, men are ranged in infinitely many degrees of virtue and knowledge. But for all of them, Buddhism tries to show the way to spiritual progress, by prescribing for them a spiritual diet suited to their individual needs. And just as it answers to the many different levels of comprehension of men, it also tries to adapt itself to the peculiarities of various cultures and races.

The Amitābha Cult

In its eagerness to satisfy the most varied needs of people, the Great Vehicle in particular has taken over many features and conceptions which were originally foreign to Buddhism. Thus in East Asia today, the cult of Buddha Amitābha is very widespread. This mythical saviour calls to his heavenly paradise all those who in their hour of death in faith seek refuge in him ; so that, being protected there from all evil influences, they can prepare themselves for Nirvāna. Here Buddhism has adopted modes of thought from the theistic religions of divine grace. But in doing so it has not abandoned its principle of an eternal cosmic law which governs everything, for Amitābha is only the bringer of good tidings into this sorrowful world. He has no part in creating or ruling it, for how could an omniscient spiritual being bring into existence this world full of pain, or hurl the wicked down into the abyss of hell for their misdeeds, or condemn them to reincarnation in miserable forms of life ?

Thus Buddhism acknowledges the differences among men in spiritual-religious matters, and has, therefore, presented its doctrine of salvation in the most variegated forms. On the other hand, it attaches no weight to differences of race, nationality, class or creed. In contrast to Brahmanism it has not excluded wide sections of the people from its gospel of salvation, and entry into its order is open to all strata of society.

(4) The fourth question which has been put to me is this : "Which social institutions belong to the foundations of mankind and which are susceptible of alteration and development without harm to what is truly human ? How does it stand in this regard with marriage, the family, the State, property, the right of self-determination of the individual, and so on ?"

According to its doctrine that all things are in a continual process of change, Buddhism recognises no social institution as eternal or unalterable. While the Chinese consider the state an institution belonging to mankind from its earliest times, Buddhism holds that it arose at a definite period of the cosmic process and will later disappear. Caste, which for the Hindus rests on God-given foundations, is for Buddhism a system arising from needs of the time, and having value only for India. Likewise marriage, the family, and property are obligatory only for worldly men of a limited historical period. With the giving up of the worldly life all these institutions lose their significance. The monk, who has renounced worldly life, has, at least in theory, risen above these obligations.

It is not surprising that this standpoint, adopted by the Buddha and by the authoritative fathers of the Buddhist church, has been much modified in the course of history. Under the pressure of outside forces, Buddhism had to make concessions to the state in several countries, and the prevailing ideal of nationalism is not without influence on the thought of many Buddhists. It is well known that in Japan among many sects loyalty to the monarch and patriotism have become articles of religious faith, and that in Tibet a kind of theocratic state has arisen.

No Central Authority

All these facts in no way alter the basic position which Buddhism adopts in relation to all earthly institutions. They have their value and their sphere of application at a certain stage ; but for those who can see everything from a higher plane, they are in themselves only temporary means whereby order is maintained in the world.

As I understand it, Buddhism is all throughout a doctrine of salvation for the individual ; the idea of a human collectivity, which has sinned and can be redeemed, is alien to it. Therefore, it has no central authority which claims the right of issuing orders or proclaiming dogmas binding on all the Buddhists of the world. When the Buddha lay on his death-bed and was asked who henceforth would lead the community, he said, "In future the Dharma will be your master."

It is clear that this pronouncement of the Exalted One had various unfortunate consequences for the community. For the absence of a generally acknowledged supreme spiritual authority had the result that very soon after the Nirvāna of the Perfect One dissensions arose over the interpretation of controversial points in the doctrine or over individual cases of monastic discipline, and that again and again new sects appeared.

Buddhism has accepted this with open eyes, for the right of self-determination of the individual and of the local congregation represented by the monastic chapter has always seemed to it to outweigh these disadvantages. How far-reaching this right of self-determination is can be seen from the fact that it not only was and is open to the layman, under certain conditions, to enter at any time into the circle of devotees of the Exalted One, and to leave it again, but it was and is even possible to belong at the same time to other religious communities and cults. The monk was always free to leave the order, and it often happened that people repeatedly during their lives became monks and returned to the world again.

In the twenty-five centuries of the history of Buddhism one naturally comes across instances in which the conditions described here have undergone modification for a time. But in general both the Lesser and the Great Vehicle have maintained the basic principle of the right of self-determination.

Buddhism and Politics

(5) The fifth question addressed to me runs as follows:

"As far as it appears possible and necessary to alter social institutions, how far and by what means is it permissible to act against the existing system and its defenders? When may co-operation be refused in the undertakings carried on by the current holders of power? When is obedience to the conventions of the society into which one was born obligatory?"

The answer to this can be given briefly. Since Buddhism tried to establish a spiritual order which is not for this world, it does not claim to be a protagonist of social reforms. It is a common error to believe that the Buddha wished to destroy the caste system in India; he did not interfere with the social order as it existed, when he laid down that caste differences should no longer be observed within his order. This was no innovation, for this principle was observed among other Indian ascetics.

To change existing conditions by violence must appear to all Buddhists completely opposed to the teaching of the Master. For any exercise of brute force is alien to the merciful spirit of the pure doctrine. The Buddha condemned any thought of hate-inspired retaliation (*Dhammapada*, 3-5).

Certainly, departures from this hallowed principle occurred, but in the whole course of Buddhist history they play no important part. It has, therefore, never known either a social revolution, nor crusades, nor wars of religion. The struggle against conditions which were found to be oppressive, and against the unrighteous claims of the mighty, was, therefore, mostly conducted in a peaceful manner by way of passive resistance.

The Perfectibility of Man

(6) The answer to the sixth question will also not occupy us long. It is as follows :

"Is man capable of changing, transforming himself, induced by instruction or revelation, and has he perhaps that capacity even to an unlimited extent ? And what are the limits of his capacity to become good and wise ?"

Buddhism does not recognise any fundamental difference between the children of light and the children of darkness, foreordained to eternal bliss or to eternal damnation. On the contrary, it assumes that there are infinitely many stages in spiritual development, and in the achievement of them, beings rise or fall in accordance with their actions performed in the course of their rebirths. The story of the robber-chief, Angulimala, who had committed many murders, shows that a man may by virtue of right instruction, evolve from a criminal to a saint in the course of one existence. Converted by the Buddha, Angulimala became an Arhat, and entered into Nirvāna.

That even the worst sinner can finally attain perfection is also shown by the story of the Buddha's cousin, Devadatta. This man committed the two worst sins known to Buddhism: he had sought, inspired by ambition, to murder the Buddha, and he had brought about a schism in the order. As punishment he died of a haemorrhage and went to hell. When he will have atoned for his misdeeds by staying in hell for a hundred thousand aeons, he will be purified of evil, and finally attain enlightenment and become a Pacceka-Buddha. The belief in man's unlimited capacity for change could hardly go farther than that.

The related question, whether all beings have the capacity, in the course of their rebirths, to become wise and good and thereby finally attain deliverance, was not answered by the Buddha. Later teachers expressed themselves on this subject in various ways. While many seem to have accepted such a belief, others* thought that there are beings who are by nature incapable of assimilating the highest knowledge, and, therefore, must remain forever subject to the cycle of rebirths.

---

*This refers to certain Mahāyāna Schools.—*The Editor.*

Buddhism and Modern Science

(7) I now turn to the seventh and last question. It runs: "How far is what contemporary science has to say about man and world in harmony with the teachings of Buddhism, or in contradiction to it?"

Buddhism originated 2,500 years ago in India, and until the beginning of the last century it was confined to countries which were entirely untouched by modern science. It therefore goes without saying that many of its doctrines, so far as they touch upon scientific, cosmological and geographical matters, are irreconcilable with the results of modern Western science. It was born and grew in an era when unlimited credulity prevailed; if we read the holy scriptures as we should read works of later times, in the spirit of literal history, we shall find things which do not fit into our modern picture of the world. We read that the Buddha was conceived by his mother miraculously, that he was able to fly through the air to Ceylon three times, that he increased food by magic, walked on water, and so on. And similar miracles are reported of his followers and of later saints; visions, magical cures, fantasies and the like, in short almost all those things which were natural to the mode of thought of antiquity and mediaeval times in all parts of the world.

A Law-governed Universe

Notwithstanding many such features, so stange to us, which like a thick undergrowth overspread more especially the later literature, we do, on the other hand, find much, even in the old texts, which strikes us as quite modern.

(a) First and above all is to be noted the principle of general and thorough-going conformity to natural law which rules the whole Buddhist system. Again and again it is said : "This basic principle stands firm, this universal conformity to law, the conditioning of one thing by another" (*Saṁyutta*, 12. 20. 4). "Profound is this law of dependent origination, Since it does not know, understand or grasp this law, this generation has become confused, like a ball of thread" (*ib.*, 12.4). But a well-trained disciple ponders thoroughly the dependent origination, for he knows thus : "When that is, this comes into being; through the destruction of that, this is destroyed" (*ib.*, 12.41-51, etc.).

(*b*) A further point of agreement is its positivistic character. For the Buddhist doctrine denies the existence of eternal substances : matter and spirit are false abstractions ; in reality there are only changing factors (*dharma*) which are lawfully connected and arise in functional dependence on each other. Like Ernst Mach, the Buddha therefore resolves the ego into a stream of lawfully co-operating elements, and can say with him : "The ego is as little an absolute permanent entity as the body. The apparent permanence of the ego consists only in its continuity."

In the philosophy of the Great Vehicle, Buddhism goes to the point of denying the reality of the external world. It is characteristic of the philosophical spirit of Asia that such epistemological doctrines do not, as with us, remain without close relation to the true religious life, but enter deeply into it and occupy the thought of wide circles. The consistent idealism of the theory of "Consciousness only" forms the basis of the Zen sect, widespread in China and Japan, which tries through meditation to realise the "void" which is above contradictions ; and it is also the basis of the priestly magic and mysticism of Tibet.

(c) It resembles modern modes of thought when the Buddha teaches that there are many problems that man, with his limited intellectual capacity, will never be able to solve, but in his cogitations about them entangles himself again and again in contradictions concerning problems such as the workings of karma, the nature of the world, the question whether the world is eternal or not, finite or infinite, how the vital principle connects with the body, and what is the state of the saint who has entered into Nirvāna.

(d) Buddhism also agrees with modern science in its picture of a universe of a vast spatial extent and unending time. The Buddha taught that there exist side by side infinitely many world systems which continually come into existence and perish again. It is not that he anticipated Copernicus ; for each world system has an earth at the centre, and sun, moon and stars revolve round it. It is rather that the conception of a multiplicity of worlds appears in his teaching as the natural consequence of the principle of retributive causality of actions. The number of actions which have to find reward or punishment is so infinitely great, that the appropriate retribution could not be comprised within one world, with its regular alternation of rising and falling cultural levels.

(e) Buddhism finds itself again in agreement with modern biology in that it acknowledges no essential difference, but only a difference of degree, between man and animal. However, it is far from the Darwinian line of thought.

(f) Finally, it can also be said that the Indians discovered the unconscious earlier than the Western psychologists. For them the unconscious consists in the totality of the impressions which slumber in the individual as the inheritance from his previous existence. The Buddhist technique of meditation, which is concerned with these latent forces, is thus a forerunner of modern psychoanalysis, of autogenic mental training, etc.

The attitudes of present-day Buddhists towards modern science vary. So far as I can see, three attitudes can be distinguished:

(*a*) The great mass of Buddhists laymen and monks in Asia are still untouched by the modern natural sciences. For them the words of the Buddha and the commentaries on them are still the infallible source of all knowledge of the universe and its phenomena.

(*b*) Many Buddhists try to prove that the cosmological ideas and miraculous stories of the Canon conform to fact, and for this purpose interpret the texts in an artificial sense or draw upon the assertions of modern occultism as proofs. It is noteworthy that they do not consider miracles to be violations of the law of nature brought about by a supernatural power, but assume that there are unknown forces and laws which cause events that to us appear as miracles but are really not.

(*c*) Other Buddhists, again, regard the statements of the texts on natural phenomena as conditioned by the ideas prevailing in those times and, therefore, no longer authoritative. They say that the Buddha was not concerned to put forward a scientific world view valid for all time, but that the essential core of Buddhism is rather its practical doctrine of salvation. The Buddha always maintained that everything of this earth is transitory, unreal and, therefore, unsatisfactory, and that so long as man is still under the subjection of the three cardinal vices of hatred, greed and ignorance he will never attain to inner peace and serene clarity of vision. Only through the purification from all desires and the complete realisation of absolute selflessness, through a moral conduct of life and constant practice of meditation, can he approach a state in which he lives in peace with himself and with the world.   Man can elevate himself and raise his stature by emulating the great example of the Buddha seated in calm meditation, whose face shines in triumphant peace. Then man can lift himself above the fierce current of time, up to the imperishable state that is beyond all the unrest of the inexorable nexus of becoming and suffering.   And the ideal that presents itself here is that unshakable composure of mind which a Buddhist verse describes :

> He whose mind is like a rock,
> Firmly anchored, shakes no more;
> Who has escaped from all passion,
> Is no more angry and no more afraid;
> He whose mind is thus without equal,
> How can sorrow defeat him ?

—Udāna, 4.4

THE WHEEL

A SERIES OF BUDDHIST PUBLICATIONS
For further reading

Vedanta and Buddhism. H. von Glasenapp (Wh 2)

Buddhism and Science. K. N. Jayatilleke, etc. (Wh 3)

The Kalāma Sutta: The Buddha's Charter of Free Inquiry, Transl. by Soma Thera (Wh 8)

Buddhism and the God Idea. Texts transl. by Nyanaponika Thera (Wh 47)

Buddhism and Comparative Religion. H. von Glasenapp (Wh 111)

Brahmanism, Buddhism and Hinduism. Lalmani Joshi (Wh 150/151)

Facets of Buddhist Thought. K. N. Jayatilleke (Wh 162/164)

Gods and the Universe. Francis Story (Wh 180/181)

The Buddhist Attitude to Other Religions. K. N. Jayatilleke (Wh 216)

Buddhism and Christianity: A Positive Approach. M. O' C. Walshe (Wh 275/276)

THE BUDDHIST PUBLICATION SOCIETY

is an approved charity dedicated to making known the Teaching of the Buddha, which has a vital message for people of all creeds.

Founded in 1958, the BPS has published a wide variety of books and booklets covering a great range of topics. Its publications include accurate annotated translations of the Buddha's discourses, standard reference works, as well as original contemporary expositions of Buddhist thought and practice. These works present Buddhism as it truly is — a dynamic force which has influenced receptive minds or the past two thousand years and is still as relevant today is it was when it first arose.

A full list of our publications will be sent free of charge upon request.

Write to :

The Hony. Secretary,
BUDDHIST PUBLICATION SOCIETY
P. O. Box 61
54, Sangharaja Mawata
Kandy — Sri Lanka